San Antonio Spurs

Richard Rambeck

CREATIVE ☾ EDUCATION

Published by Creative Education
123 South Broad Street, Mankato, Minnesota 56001
Creative Education is an imprint of The Creative Company

Designed by Rita Marshall

Photos by: Allsport Photography, Associated Press/Wide World Photos, Focus on Sports, NBA Photos, UPI/Corbis-Bettmann, and SportsChrome.

Photo page 1: Sean Elliott
Photo title page: Dominique Wilkins

Library of Congress Cataloging-in-Publication Data

Rambeck, Richard.
San Antonio Spurs / Richard Rambeck.
p. cm. — (NBA today)
Summary: Describes the background and history of the San Antonio Spurs pro basketball team to 1997.
ISBN 0-88682-890-2

1. San Antonio Spurs (Basketball team)—Juvenile literature.
[1. San Antonio Spurs (Basketball team)—History. 2. Basketball—History.]
I. Title. II. Series: NBA today (Mankato, Minn.)

GV885.52.S26R36 1997   96-52962
796.323'64'09764351—dc21

First edition

5 4 3 2

San Antonio began as a small Spanish mission on the vast plains of Texas. In 1836, San Antonio de Valero, a mission also known as the Alamo, played an important role in United States history. One hundred and eighty courageous Americans tried to halt the advancement into Texas of Mexican general Santa Anna and his army of 5,000 soldiers. Led by Davy Crockett and Jim Bowie, the Americans held off the Mexican army for two weeks before the Alamo fell and nearly all of its defenders were killed.

Several weeks later, American general Sam Houston launched a counterattack against Santa Anna's forces in the

Swen Nater was an original Spur.

John Beasley was voted the ABA All-Star Game's MVP.

Battle of San Jacinto. "Remember the Alamo!" the Americans cried as they defeated the Mexican army, declaring independence for the state of Texas.

Within a few years, San Antonio had become a great western outpost. Today it is one of the 10 largest cities in the United States. With a population of more than one million people, the proud city has more than doubled in size in the last 40 years.

Residents still speak with pride of the courage displayed by the brave men who fought at the Alamo mission. "Visitors to San Antonio may get the feeling that the city's residents all trace their ancestry to someone who fought on one side or the other at that mission," wrote a local historian.

But preserving history isn't the only activity in the city. Residents also devote themselves to rooting for San Antonio's only major-league professional sports team, the San Antonio Spurs of the National Basketball Association (NBA). Since 1973, the Spurs have thrilled local fans with high-scoring, exciting play. In fact, the team had only two losing seasons during the first 16 years of its existence, and with current stars David Robinson, Dominique Wilkins, and Chuck Person, they hope to finally bring a championship to San Antonio.

THE SPURS ROUND UP VICTORIOUS SEASONS

The initial years of the Spurs franchise weren't spent in San Antonio, but in nearby Dallas. The team, founded in 1967, was named the Dallas Chaparrals, or "Chaps." One of the charter members of the American Basketball Association

All-Star Artis Gilmore.

(ABA), the Chaps were one of the better teams in the league, but the residents of Dallas didn't seem to notice. Sometimes fewer than 500 people attended the club's home games.

Most of Dallas never saw the fine play of player/coach Cliff Hagan, a former NBA All-Star, or of forward John Beasley, a fine rebounder and scorer who was the Most Valuable Player of the 1968–69 ABA All-Star Game. Hagan and Beasley were joined by guards Ron Boone and Glen Combs, both outstanding outside shooters. In the 1969–70 season, Dallas finished second in the Western Division, but the team still hadn't gained a following.

The owners tried everything to make the Chaps a success. They changed the team name to the Texas Chaparrals and played home games in Dallas, Fort Worth, and Lubbock in an attempt to gain statewide support for the team. But the changes only hurt what little support the club already had.

Finally, after the 1972–73 season, the Chaps were sold to colorful Texas millionaire Red McCombs. He moved the club to San Antonio and changed its name to the Spurs. The team, which had always been a success on the court, soon became a success at the box office as well. "We made a few key deals, won some games, and suddenly we were drawing a crowd," recalled San Antonio general manager John Begzos. "We were stunned. People figured we were geniuses, but we didn't even know what we were doing."

1 9 7 4

The Chaparrals nabbed a future star when they signed free agent James Silas.

THE ICEMAN HEATS THINGS UP IN SAN ANTONIO

Begzos may not have been clear about what the team was doing, but the Spurs were clearly headed in the right direction when they bought the contracts of 7-foot center Swen Nater and 6-foot-8 forward George Gervin from the troubled Virginia Squires. San Antonio spent $300,000 for Nater and $250,000 for Gervin, but it was Gervin who really paid off for the Spurs. At only 20 years old, Gervin became San Antonio's leading scorer. The skinny forward was as cool as ice on the court; he was so calm, in fact, that he had been given the nickname "Iceman" by his teammates in Virginia.

Swen Nater's 1,279 rebounds and 16.4 rebound average still stand as Spurs records.

From the beginning, the Iceman was a hot commodity for the Spurs. He poured in 23 points a game by hitting shots from all over the court. Sometimes he didn't even bother to look at the hoop before he shot. "I don't really have to look at the basket," he told reporters after one game. "It's just a feeling I get. I know where I'm standing on the court, and that tells me how to shoot the ball."

Gervin had grown up in a Detroit ghetto. He learned how to shoot on a back-alley court behind his cousin's house. "It was a poverty area," Gervin recalled. "There was trash and rats, but there was nowhere else to go. We dodged the trash and stayed out of the way of the rats. I just wanted to play basketball."

Gervin became a star at Martin Luther King High School in Detroit. After high school, he enrolled at California State University at Long Beach for a short time, but soon left to attend Eastern Michigan University. Gervin didn't last long at Eastern Michigan, either; he was suspended from the team for punching an opposing player. No college would touch him after that, so Gervin wound up playing in a semi-pro league in Pontiac, Michigan. One night, Gervin scored 50 points in

George Gervin, the "Iceman."

Alvin Robertson was another high-flying Spur.

a game. Luckily for him, there were several ABA scouts watching him from the sidelines.

Soon afterwards, in 1972, Gervin signed with the Virginia Squires, where he played in the shadow of Julius Erving for a season and a half. His big break came when the Spurs bought his contract during his second year in Virginia. Gervin came to San Antonio as an unknown, but that didn't worry him. "I just do my thing and stay consistent," Gervin explained. "I figure the people will be recognizing the Iceman pretty soon now."

Gervin led the Spurs to at least 50 victories in both 1974–75 and 1975-76. Although they didn't win a championship either season, the Spurs were one of the best teams in the ABA. They also were one of the best supported.

In 1976, the NBA and ABA agreed to merge. As a result,

1 9 7 6

In their first NBA game, Doug Moe led the Spurs to a 121-118 victory over the 76ers.

All-Star guard James Silas.

four ABA teams—San Antonio, the New Jersey Nets, the Indiana Pacers, and the Denver Nuggets—were added to the list of NBA squads. The Spurs, led by Gervin, surprised other teams in their new league by making the playoffs after the 1976–77 season. The following year, Gervin won the league scoring title. The skinny Spur was now the most dangerous scorer in the NBA.

George Gervin scored 63 points on the last day of the season to win the NBA scoring title.

"To stop Ice, you have to beat Ice up," said San Antonio guard George Karl. "That worked in the past, but now he knows he's going to get slapped and bumped every time he goes for the shot. So it doesn't bother him."

Gervin became even more dangerous when San Antonio coach Doug Moe moved him from forward to guard. The 6-foot-8 Gervin was just too tall for the shorter guards to handle; he ended up winning the league scoring title three years in a row. With the game on the line, the ball was almost always in Gervin's possession. "I consider the game won when Ice has his hands on the ball in that situation," said San Antonio center Billy Paultz.

The Iceman, Paultz, forward Larry Kenon, and guard Mike Gale all helped deliver two Central Division titles to San Antonio in 1977–78 and 1978–79. The 1978–79 team advanced to the Eastern Conference championship series, but lost to the Washington Bullets.

Despite their success, the Spurs were about to go through a series of changes. Coach Moe was replaced by Stan Albeck after the 1979–80 season. In addition, the team was moved from the NBA Central Division to the Midwest Division, which is in the Western Conference. These changes had little effect: the Spurs remained a high-scoring, fast-breaking team, winning division titles in both 1980–81 and 1981–82. Each time, though, San Antonio was eliminated in the second round of the playoffs. Other changes were clearly needed for the Spurs to reach the top of the NBA.

SPURS ADD ARTIS FOR TITLE RUN

1 9 8 0

All-Star Larry Kenon topped the Spurs in rebounding for the fifth consecutive season.

Albeck and the team management decided that the Iceman needed some help—some big help. So the Spurs traded power forward Mark Olberding and center Dave Corzine to the Chicago Bulls for 7-foot-2 center Artis Gilmore. Gilmore was one of the oldest players in the league, but he was also one of the biggest and strongest. He had been a standout for the Kentucky Colonels of the ABA during the early 1970s. After the ABA and NBA merged and the Kentucky franchise folded, Gilmore was picked up by the Chicago Bulls in 1976. While with Chicago, Gilmore made the NBA All-Star team three times and established himself as one of the best centers in the league.

Chicago coach Jerry Sloan recalled a game in which Gilmore had scored 25 points, grabbed 15 rebounds, and blocked 5 shots. "But even more than that was the way he intimidated people," Sloan said. "The way players came to the middle, saw him, and traveled or threw the ball away. I remember Artis going the length of the court and catching a guy from behind and blocking his shot. Those are things that mean more than points."

Gilmore had his critics, however. Some said he was too slow and too nice to be a great player. One sportswriter called him "Kareem [Abdul-Jabbar] without moves." Gilmore

Power forward Mark Olberding.

Tough defense has been a trademark of the club.

knew he wasn't the player Abdul-Jabbar was. "The difference between Kareem and me is that he's got one incredible offensive weapon—the skyhook. It's unstoppable. I don't have anything like that," he noted.

The Spurs, however, believed Gilmore had enough weapons, both on offense and defense, to allow them to contend for a championship. Coach Stan Albeck was convinced that he couldn't win a league crown without a great center. Now he had his big man and Gervin, too, who won his fourth scoring title in 1981–82.

In the 1982–83 season, Gervin and Gilmore gave the Spurs a one-two punch that resulted in 53 victories—a team record. San Antonio also claimed its third straight Midwest Division title and fifth division championship in six years. The Spurs then won two playoff series and advanced to the Western Conference Finals against the Los Angeles Lakers. Los Angeles, led by Magic Johnson, ended San Antonio's title dreams and went on to win the NBA championship.

After the devastating loss to the Lakers, the Spurs went into a tailspin. Albeck left to coach the New Jersey Nets. Gilmore was injured and missed two months of the following season. Gervin, who was starting to show signs of age, couldn't carry the team alone. The Spurs stumbled to their worst record ever. They finished 37–45 and missed the playoffs for the first time since joining the NBA. It was time to rebuild.

1 9 8 1

George Johnson made his first of two consecutive playoff appearances, contributing 31 points.

The Spurs establish position (pages 18–19).

1 9 8 5

Johnny Moore made 229 steals, ranking second in the NBA.

As the Spurs slipped, so did Gervin. His scoring average dropped several points a game, and he wasn't the player he had been. Before the 1985–86 season began, team management decided it was time to part ways with the Iceman, and he was traded to the Chicago Bulls.

The main reason the Spurs could afford to deal Gervin away was the play of second-year guard Alvin Robertson, from the University of Arkansas. A great athlete who could play superb defense, Robertson was also able to make several steals a game. "The Spurs were always known as a high-scoring offensive team led by Ice," San Antonio coach Cotton Fitzsimmons explained, "but we needed toughness and quickness. Alvin gave us that look."

The legendary George Gervin.

Robertson, who played on the 1984 U.S. Olympic team, made it clear he wasn't another Gervin. "I can't be like Ice, and I'm not trying to be," Robertson said. "When I met him, he was so smooth, so calm. He's still the main man around here. Nothing will change that. But, honestly, I felt I outplayed him every time in the [1985–86] preseason. Every time. That's just the way it was."

Robertson not only took Gervin's place in the lineup, but he was also chosen by the fans to start in the 1986 All-Star Game. It was a remarkable achievement for a second-year player, especially one who was best known for his defense. Robertson averaged 17 points, 6.3 rebounds, and 5.5 assists per game in 1985–86, and his 301 steals marked a single-season league record. The Spurs guard was named the NBA's Most Improved Player and Defensive Player of the Year.

1 9 8 6

Guard Johnny Dawkins was the Spurs' first pick in the college draft.

ROBINSON ATTRACTS ATTENTION

Despite Robertson's heroics, the Spurs still were not a good team. The 1986–87 squad finished with a 28–54 record. San Antonio didn't make the playoffs, but the Spurs did gain the first pick in the 1987 draft. They used it to take David Robinson, the 7-foot-1 center from the United States Naval Academy who had been the 1987 College Player of the Year.

Even though Robinson was the best player in that draft, the Spurs were taking a gamble in picking him. Because Robinson went to college at the Naval Academy, he couldn't move on to the NBA immediately after graduating. First he

The talented Willie Anderson.

had to serve his country, perhaps for as long as five years. As it turned out, the Navy agreed to let Robinson go after two years of full-time service. The Spurs drafted him in 1987, knowing that he couldn't play until the 1989–90 season. The team's officials were willing to be patient because they knew that Robinson was worth waiting for.

While Robinson was fulfilling his two-year commitment to the Navy, the Spurs won only 52 of 164 games during the 1987–88 and 1988–89 seasons. Their coach was proven winner Larry Brown, who took the job knowing the Spurs would not be a good team until Robinson traded in his Navy uniform for the black and white outfit of San Antonio. Brown's team didn't have much all-around talent, but guard Willie Anderson and forward Greg Anderson soon matured into solid players, as did point guard Johnny Dawkins.

Robinson's naval duty ended in the summer of 1989, but that didn't mean that the Spurs' rebuilding process was over. Because Brown and team management knew that the center would not be able to turn the franchise around all by himself, they made some strategic moves. First, San Antonio used the third pick in the 1989 draft to take Sean Elliott, a talented forward from the University of Arizona. Next, the team made several key trades. Alvin Robertson and Greg Anderson went to the Milwaukee Bucks for veteran forward Terry Cummings. Johnny Dawkins was dealt to the Philadelphia 76ers for veteran point guard Maurice Cheeks. San Antonio's strategy was clear: the team was counting on Cheeks and Cummings to help guide such young talents as Willie Anderson, Sean Elliott, and David Robinson.

The big center's first game with the Spurs was on July 25,

Greg "Cadillac" Anderson placed second in the voting for NBA Rookie of the Year.

Willie Anderson led the Spurs in scoring and was second in rebounds and assists.

1989. It was an intrasquad scrimmage played in front of a large crowd. Robinson proved right away that he was the best player on the floor. He gave the cheering fans their money's worth by scoring 31 points, grabbing 17 rebounds, and blocking 10 shots.

Four months later, the Spurs opened the season at home against the powerful Los Angeles Lakers. Robinson scored 23 points and had 17 rebounds during that contest, and San Antonio won 106–98. The San Antonio center was a star from the very beginning. "Some rookies are never really rookies. Robinson's one of them," said Los Angeles All-Star guard Magic Johnson. "If he's still learning the game, I'd hate to see him when he knows it cold," said New Jersey guard Mookie Blaylock.

"He has the talent all us big guys only hope and dream for," said San Antonio backup center Caldwell Jones. "No other big guy I've ever seen is anywhere near as quick and fast as he is. That's what sets David apart."

Led by Robinson, the Spurs became the surprise team in the league. The previous season, San Antonio had finished second to last in the Midwest Division. In 1989–90, the Spurs captured first place. Robinson was the main reason they went from losers to winners so fast. He finished the season with a scoring average of 24.3 points per game, tenth best in the NBA. To no one's surprise, Robinson was named the NBA's Rookie of the Year. He was also selected for the second team of the league's All-Defensive squad.

an Antonio ended the 1989–90 season with a 56–26 record. The Spurs beat Denver in the first round of the playoffs and then faced Portland in the second round. The clubs split the first six games. In the seventh and deciding contest, San Antonio led, 97–90, late in the fourth quarter. But the young Spurs couldn't hold the lead. The Trail Blazers scored the last seven points of the fourth period to force the game into overtime.

Rod Strickland had a team-leading average of eight assists per game.

In the extra period, with the score tied 103–103, young Spurs point guard Rod Strickland made a costly mistake. Strickland, who had come from the New York Knicks in a trade for Maurice Cheeks, tried an over-the-head pass to Elliott that was intercepted by Portland's Jerome Kersey. Portland went on to score and win the game. Strickland's play showed that the youthful Spurs still had some growing up to do.

The following year, San Antonio won the Midwest Division again. Robinson had another outstanding year, as did Sean Elliott, who was blossoming into one of the better small forwards in the NBA. Even so, the Spurs fell to the Golden State Warriors in the first round of the playoffs.

This pattern of doing well in the regular season while not being quite good enough to advance through the playoffs became the yearly routine for San Antonio throughout the 1990s. George Gervin had never been able to win a championship all on his own, and it looked as if David Robinson was faring no better.

Coach Brown—never one to stay with a sinking ship—

Top-scoring center David Robinson (pages 26–27).

*Sean Elliott
represented the
Spurs in the NBA
All-Star Game.*

must have sensed something was wrong in San Antonio. He quit midway through the 1991–92 season. The Spurs made it to the playoffs without Brown, but Robinson had undergone hand surgery and was unavailable in the postseason. Without the "Admiral" (Robinson's nickname, referring to his Naval service) the Spurs lost to Phoenix in the first round.

Under new coach John Lucas, the Admiral and his teammates made the playoffs again the following year. Robinson's all-around play carried the Spurs through a close first-round series against the Portland Trail Blazers. In the second round, the Spurs faced Phoenix again. Late in game six, with Phoenix up three games to two, the score was tied, 100–100. The Suns' Charles Barkley broke the tie with 1.8 seconds left on the clock. Robinson took the last shot of the game, but missed, and the Spurs' season was over.

The loss convinced Spurs management to get Robinson some help. Before the 1993–94 season, Sean Elliott was traded to the Pistons for Dennis Rodman, a defensive specialist and the NBA's top rebounder. The Spurs, set to play their first season in the brand new Alamodome, were like a brand new team with the addition of Rodman. A tough competitor in Detroit, Rodman remained tough when he moved to San Antonio, but he became flashy, too. He dyed his hair different colors throughout the season—white, red, green—which caught the attention of spectators across the country. But it was Rodman's effect on Robinson that was getting the attention of Spurs fans in particular.

With Rodman's rebounding skills, Robinson was able to concentrate on scoring. Rodman also encouraged the Admiral to get tough, and Robinson did. They became the first teammates to lead the NBA in both scoring (Robinson) and rebounding (Rodman) in the same season. But after Robinson and Rodman were unable to carry the Spurs past the Utah Jazz in the first round of the playoffs, Coach Lucas quit. He was replaced by Bob Hill.

The Hill-led Spurs went 62–20 in 1994–95, the best record in franchise history. Robinson was named the NBA's Most Valuable Player, and Rodman led the league in rebounding, even though he missed 33 games. In the playoffs, the Spurs beat the Denver Nuggets and Los Angeles Lakers before losing to the Houston Rockets in the conference finals. Though the Spurs lost, it looked as if they were ready to contend for a championship. But then Rodman was traded to the Chicago Bulls in the off-season for center Will Perdue, and it looked like it was once again all up to the Admiral.

Dennis Rodman was selected to the NBA All-Defensive First Team.

The multitalented Vinny Del Negro.

Avery Johnson, the Spurs' confident point guard. 31

Venezuelan Carl Herrera scored a career-high 24 points in a game against the Bucks.

Robinson's teammates, however, stepped up. A cast that included Perdue, Chuck Person, Sean Elliott—who had returned to the Spurs—and Charles Smith ended the 1995–96 regular season with 59 wins. It looked as though the Admiral and his crew had finally put things together. But the Spurs performed poorly against Utah in the first round of the playoffs, losing game six and the series by an embarrassing final score of 108–81.

The Spurs swore that the playoff defeat was a fluke, and they planned to make their run at the championship in 1996–97, proving their critics wrong. But Robinson spent much of the season injured and on the bench, along with Person, Smith, and newcomer Dominique Wilkins, who, when healthy, managed to become the team's leader, showing flashes of his former All-Star self. Team management fired Hill early in the season—even though his top stars hadn't been on the court—and general manager Gregg Popovich became the new coach. But he was hampered all season long by injuries to his key players, and by the season's end, the mantra in San Antonio had become "if we're healthy, we'll win." The Spurs aren't looking to bring in expensive free agents or top draft picks—all they want is to bring a strong team to the floor night after night. Both fans and players know that a healthy team may be all it takes for the Spurs to bring home a San Antonio championship in the very near future.